Shakespeare's W

Theatre and Entertainment

Kathy Elgin

CHERRYTREE BOOKS

Titles in this series:
Daily Life
Crime and Punishment
Health and Disease
Theatre and Entertainment

Copyright © 2005 Bailey Publishing
Associates Ltd

Produced for Evans Brothers by
Bailey Publishing Associates Ltd
11a Woodlands
Hove BN3 6TJ

Editor: Alex Woolf
Designer: Simon Borrough
Artwork: Adam Hook
Picture research: Glass Onion Pictures

Published in Great Britain by Cherrytree
Books, part of the Evans Publishing Group.

British Library Cataloguing in Publication
Data
Elgin, Kathy, 1948-
   Theatre and Entertainment. -
(Shakespeare's World)
   1. Shakespeare, William 1564-1616 -
Themes, motives - Juvenile literature
   2. Theatre - England - History - 16th
century - Juvenile literature
   3. England - Social life and customs -
16th century - Juvenile literature
   I. Title
   792', 0942'09031

ISBN 1 842 34189 8

Printed and bound in China

Evans Brothers Ltd
2a Portman Mansions,
Chiltern Street
London W1U 6NR

Picture Acknowledgements:
The publishers would like to thank the
following for permission to reproduce
their pictures:
Art Archive: cover (both), 4, 7, 8, 9, 13
(both), 27; Bridgeman Art Library: 6, 11
(bottom), 15, 17, 18, 19, 21 (bottom),
22, 23, 25 (both), 29 (both); Pictorial
Press: 11 (top); Shakespeare's Globe
Picture Library: 21 (top); Topham: 14,
16; Victoria & Albert Museum: 26.

Contents

Introduction

Who Was Shakespeare?

William Shakespeare is probably the most famous playwright in the world. He was born in 1564 in Stratford-upon-Avon, and four hundred years after his death his plays are still being performed all over the world in almost every language you can think of. Although he came from a fairly ordinary family and didn't even go to university, he wrote thirty-eight plays with exciting plots and new, dramatic language.

Most of his plays were performed at the Globe, one of the very first theatres in London. Some were also performed for Queen Elizabeth I herself at court. Because he was also an actor and probably appeared in some of his own plays, Shakespeare knew what audiences liked. He became one of the most popular playwrights of his day and, by the time he died in 1616, he was a wealthy man.

Theatre and Entertainment in Shakespeare's Time

The Elizabethans, from Queen Elizabeth herself right down to the poorest villagers, loved to be entertained. Sometimes this meant sitting in an audience, sometimes taking part themselves in theatricals, dressing up, playing or listening to music, and dancing. Rich people at court lived their whole lives as a kind of performance. Even their ordinary clothing was so elaborate that it often looked like fancy dress.

The newest and most fashionable kind of entertainment was the theatre, to which people flocked in their thousands. Until then acting had been a rather amateur affair, but in Shakespeare's time it became a real profession.

Shakespeare was so involved with theatre that he couldn't help writing about it. In all his plays he uses images and language drawn from the theatre and other forms of entertainment. Several of his plays — *A Midsummer Night's Dream*, *Hamlet* and *Love's Labour's Lost* — have scenes in which actors perform a play within the play. This gives Shakespeare the opportunity to write about costumes, different styles of acting, plays by other writers and so on, which of course gives us a lot of information about the theatre of his time.

He also uses his own early life in Stratford-upon-Avon to tell us about the very different kinds of entertainment enjoyed by people in country areas. Characters in his plays go hunting, play bowls, keep greyhounds and enjoy themselves just as he saw people doing all around him.

The Theatres

Plays used to be performed by travelling groups of actors who set up temporary stages in towns and villages. By about 1570, however, permanent theatres were being built in London to meet the popular demand for drama. People flocked in their thousands to the Theatre, the Curtain, the Rose, the Swan and the Globe. All theatres had to be built outside the city boundary, and several were built on the south bank of the Thames, which made going to the theatre an exciting excursion.

The Swan Theatre

The Globe Theatre

A view of the Thames in 1616 shows the Globe and Swan theatres on the south bank, with St Paul's Cathedral opposite.

cockpit: the theatre, similar in shape to the pit where cock-fighting was held
vasty: vast
casques: helmets
affright: frighten

... *Can this cockpit hold*
The vasty fields of France? Or may we cram
Within this wooden O the very casques
That did affright the air at Agincourt?
HENRY V, ACT I, PROLOGUE

The "wooden O" is a good description of the public theatres. They were large, round timber buildings with an open space in the middle surrounded by galleries of seats. The stage projected into the central space, with a building behind it containing dressing rooms. The gallery roof was usually thatched, which made fire a constant hazard. The first Globe burned down after sparks from a stage cannon set light to the thatch.

Groundlings (people who stood in front of the stage) often ate and drank throughout performances.

A model of Shakespeare's Globe. The theatre was reconstructed close to the original site in the 1990s.

> *O, it offends me to the soul to hear a robustious periwig-pated fellow tear a passion to tatters ... to split the ears of the groundlings, who for the most part are capable of nothing but inexplicable dumb-shows and noise.*
>
> HAMLET, ACT 3, SCENE 2

robustious: boisterous, noisy
periwig-pated: wearing a wig
capable of: appreciative of

The better-off people sat in proper seats in the galleries, where they could show themselves off as well as watch the play. For a penny, poorer people could stand in the space in front of the stage. These were the "groundlings" Hamlet is making fun of. They were famous for their rowdy behaviour. Caught up in the excitement of the play, they often joined in, shouting out comments and sometimes climbing on the stage.

How Theatres were Organized

Theatre companies were cooperatives. Perhaps a dozen members, usually actors, shared the financial costs and the profits, as well as the responsibility of running the theatre. They were known as the "sharers". The most important aim was to secure a noble patron whose name the company would carry. After first joining the Queen's Men, Shakespeare became a founder member of the Lord Chamberlain's Men, renamed the King's Men when James I came to the throne. He remained with the company for most of his life.

> In the meantime I will draw a bill of properties, such as our play wants.
> A MIDSUMMER NIGHT'S DREAM, ACT 1, SCENE 2

properties: small items needed on stage
wants: needs

This sixteenth-century drawing shows us the inside of the Swan Theatre, with some actors on the stage.

Between them the sharers owned the costumes, props and playscripts. Peter Quince, the one speaking here, is in charge of the properties, and is also the "bookholder" for the performance, which was the nearest thing to a director in Elizabethan theatre. He organized rehearsals and made sure the actors knew their lines. As well as the main sharers, other actors were hired as needed for individual plays. The company also needed stagehands, wardrobe keepers and musicians.

> *Speak the speech, I pray you,*
> *as I pronounced it to you,*
> *trippingly on the tongue; but if*
> *you mouth it as many of your*
> *players do, I had as lief the*
> *town-crier spoke my lines.*
> HAMLET, ACT 3, SCENE 2

trippingly: nimbly, fluently
mouth it: speak it
lief: rather

GLOBE. SOUTHWARKE.

The plays were a company's most valuable assets and were closely guarded. Scribes wrote out copies of each actor's part. Shakespeare was chief playwright of his company and had to produce at least two new plays a year, as well as revising old ones. Some plays stayed in the repertoire for years and were performed regularly. The Stationer's Register kept a record of all the plays performed.

As many as three thousand people crowded in to each performance at the Globe.

Actors only had a few days to learn their parts and sometimes they improvised a little.

Elizabethan Plays

The new permanent theatres allowed writers to produce more sophisticated plays. They could now include spectacular effects and suggest different locations. Certain types of play became fashionable at different times. For example, when Shakespeare began to write, plays about revenge and supernatural events involving ghosts were all the rage. Shakespeare was clever enough to follow the fashion, but his plays were better than the others because he made his characters more interesting by showing what they were thinking.

Playwrights were not rich men. The writers of one play in 1599 were paid £8, while a single costume for the same play cost £10.

The best actors in the world, either for tragedy, comedy, history, pastoral, pastoral-comical, historical-pastoral, tragical-historical, tragical-comical-historical-pastoral ...
HAMLET, ACT 2, SCENE 2

pastoral: set in the country

Theatre companies had to be able to perform a wide variety of plays. Tragedies were serious dramas about the downfall of heroes, usually including murder and revenge. Comedies weren't necessarily funny, but just light-hearted plays with happy endings. Pastoral plays showed the simple lives of shepherds and farmers. As more people left the countryside to live in towns, they became nostalgic for this old way of life. Especially popular in wartime were plays based on real historical events. Being reminded of the exploits of the great King Henry V, for example, made English people feel patriotic.

> *If this were played*
> *upon a stage now, I*
> *should condemn it as*
> *an improbable fiction.*
> TWELFTH NIGHT,
> ACT 3, SCENE 4

Elizabethan theatre was, above all, great entertainment. Even serious plays included songs and dances to break up the action and please the groundlings. Audiences loved to be scared by supernatural elements like ghosts, witches and magicians, and grisly murders were a frequent feature. It was also quite usual for playwrights to recycle plots from earlier plays or from published stories. Shakespeare borrowed material from all kinds of sources, especially translations of foreign tales.

The Spanish Tragedy:

OR,

HIERONIMO is mad againe.

Containing the lamentable end of *Don Horatio,* and *Belimperia*; With the pitifull Death of HIERONIMO.

Newly Corrected, Amended, and Enlarged with new Additions, as it hath of late beene divers times Acted.

LONDON
Printed by *Augustine Mathewes,* for *Francis Grove,* and are to bee sold at his Shoppe, neere the Sarazens Head, upon Snovy-hill. 1633.

This film of Henry V, about the English victory over the French at Agincourt (1415), was made during the Second World War. It was shown to British soldiers to raise morale.

As its title page shows, Thomas Kyd's The Spanish Tragedy *was full of the sensational events audiences loved, including madness and several murders.*

Shakespeare's Plays

Shakespeare wrote many different kinds of play. He began by dramatizing historical episodes like the Wars of the Roses. These were very popular because they had exciting battle scenes and brought to life events that everyone had heard about. He also wrote light-hearted plays full of squabbling lovers, mistaken identity and lively, witty heroines. Later came the great tragedies like *King Lear* and *Macbeth*, and his last plays were romances, full of strange magic, in which mistakes are put right and lost treasures are found.

O'erstep not the modesty of nature. For anything so o'er-done is from the purpose of playing, whose end both at the first and now, was and is to hold as t'were the mirror up to nature.
HAMLET, ACT 3, SCENE 2

O'erstep: exceed
modesty: discipline, moderation
from: remote from

Shakespeare knew that the best kind of theatre involved characters which the audience could recognize as people like themselves. In the old drama, performances had been stylized, with actors reciting plodding poetry and making stock gestures. Shakespeare wanted actors to behave more naturally on stage and to speak realistically. Although he was a poet, he often wrote in prose, which was quite new.

A Midsummer Night's Dream, *in which a character gets transformed into a donkey, is one of Shakespeare's most popular plays.*

All the world's a stage,
And all the men and women merely players:
They have their exits and their entrances;
And one man in his time plays many parts.
As You Like It, Act 2, Scene 7

*The title page from the first
collected edition of Shakespeare's
plays, published in 1623.*

This character reminds us that theatre and real life are quite
similar: we play many different parts as we grow up.
Shakespeare often used his own experience in his plays.
Characters like Puck and Titania come from the old tales
and fairy stories of
Warwickshire, where he
grew up. And his
knowledge of theatre and
acting comes out in
many of his own works,
which feature plays
within plays, including
Hamlet and *A Midsummer
Night's Dream.*

The Merry Wives of Windsor,
*with its fat hero Falstaff, was
one of Queen Elizabeth's
favourites and may have been
written especially for her.*

and their entrances; And one man in his time plays many parts.

13

Other Playwrights

We now think of Shakespeare as the greatest playwright of his day, but of course there were many others. Public demand for new plays encouraged a flood of ambitious new writers, all determined to make a reputation. In 1594, the company at the Rose theatre performed thirty-eight plays in one season, twenty-one of which were completely new! Some playwrights of that era were more popular than Shakespeare, but their work is now quite forgotten. Others have survived.

Marlowe's hero Tamburlaine, played here by Sir Antony Sher, was based on a fourteenth-century warrior who conquered half the known world.

> *How many ages hence*
> *Shall this our lofty scene be acted over*
> *In states unborn and accents yet*
> *unknown.*
>
> JULIUS CAESAR, ACT 3,
> SCENE 1

hence: in the future

Of the playwrights whose work survives, Shakespeare's most serious rival was Christopher Marlowe. He wrote epic plays such as *Tamburlaine the Great*, full of heroic action and dramatic verse. Thomas Kyd is famous for starting the fashion for revenge dramas with his play *The Spanish Tragedy*, and John Webster continued this theme, thrilling audiences with plays full of gruesome murders. Ben Jonson, who was Shakespeare's friend as well as a rival, wrote satirical comedies poking fun at greedy modern society.

In a long career, Ben Jonson wrote poetry and masques as well as plays.

The play's the thing
Wherein I'll catch the
conscience of the king.
HAMLET, ACT 2,
SCENE 2

*Christopher
Marlowe was
suspected of being a
spy and his career was cut
short when he was stabbed
during a fight in a tavern.*

Writing a play for one of these theatres was rather like writing a screenplay for a Hollywood film today. Educated people may have admired individual writers but most Elizabethan audiences were generally more interested in the play than in its author. Managers, only interested in new, up-to-the-minute material, employed and dismissed writers as they needed them. Often several writers worked on the same project, either re-writing each other's work or each writing the bits they were good at. Most Elizabethan playwrights, including Shakespeare, worked together in various combinations at one time or another.

The Actors

Although they were regarded with suspicion by the authorities, actors were, on the whole, respectable and reasonably educated people. As there were no drama schools, they learned their craft on stage. Shakespeare joined the theatre as an actor and probably went on performing on and off while he was writing. One of his roles was Old Adam, the family servant in *As You Like It*. Ben Jonson also began his career as an actor, although apparently a very bad one.

> *Life's but a walking shadow, a poor player*
> *That struts and frets his hour upon the stage,*
> *And then is heard no more.*
>
> MACBETH, ACT 5, SCENE 6

Macbeth here reminds us that an actor's performance is soon over and forgotten. Nevertheless, some Elizabethan actors became great celebrities. Audiences saw actors regularly in a variety of roles and liked to pick out their favourites. The two greatest tragic actors were Edward Alleyn of the Admiral's Men and Richard Burbage of Shakespeare's company. Shakespeare almost certainly wrote the roles of Hamlet, Othello and King Lear for Burbage, and he was especially famous for his performance as Richard III.

Edward Alleyn retired from the stage early and became a wealthy businessman.

16

> And let those that play your clowns
> speak no more than is set down for
> them — for there be of them that will
> themselves laugh, to set on some quan-
> tity of barren spectators to laugh too...
>
> HAMLET, ACT 3, SCENE 2

*Will Kemp, another clown
in Shakespeare's company,
was famous for dancing a
nine-day morris dance all
the way from London
to Norwich.*

Hamlet warns the company's comic actors not to
spoil scenes, as they often did, by
fooling about or adding extra jokes
to get a laugh. Shakespeare
probably had Richard Tarleton in
mind, the famous clown for whom
he had written many great comedy
routines. Tarleton had been a solo
performer and sometimes forgot he was
now part of a company with a script to follow.
Tarleton was Queen Elizabeth's favourite, until
he upset her by making jokes about the Earl of
Leicester. Theatre and politics could be a
dangerous mixture!

*The role of Hamlet is one of
the most difficult because it
combines tragedy and
pretended madness.*

Boy Actors

Because women were not allowed to act on stage, all the female roles had to be performed by boys whose voices had not yet broken. Playing a young girl like Juliet may not have been too difficult, but Shakespeare's older heroines, such as Cleopatra, or Rosalind in *As You Like It*, must have taken a lot of skill. When they joined a company, boys learned their trade by being apprenticed to older actors.

10 The Roaring Girle.
OR
Moll Cut-Purse.

As it hath lately beene Acted on the Fortune-stage by
the Prince his Players.

Written by *T. Middleton* and *T. Dekkar*.

My case is alter'd, I must worke for my liuing.

Printed at *London* for *Thomas Archer*, and are to be sold at his
shop in Popes head-pallace, neere the Royall
Exchange. 1611.

The title page of a play written in 1611 by Thomas Dekker and Thomas Middleton. A boy of about fourteen would have played Moll Cutpurse, a real-life female pickpocket who dressed as a man.

Nay, faith, let not me play a woman: I have a beard coming.

A MIDSUMMER NIGHT'S DREAM,
ACT 1, SCENE 2

Francis Flute here is dismayed at being cast as the heroine in the play. He tries to get out of it by saying he is old enough to shave. But boys didn't only play female characters. Shakespeare also wrote excellent children's roles, like William in *The Merry Wives of Windsor*. Having boys play women also gave playwrights the chance to write funny plots in which female characters have to disguise themselves as boys. The audience is then watching a boy playing a girl who is pretending to be a boy.

the fashion, and so berattle the common

> *There is, sir, an eyrie of children, little eyases, that cry out on the top of question, and are most tyrannically clapped for't. These are now the fashion, and so berattle the common stages...*
>
> HAMLET, ACT 3, SCENE 2

eyrie: nest
eyases: young hawks
on the top of question: with maximum force
tyrannically: forcefully
berattle: fill with noise
common stages: public playhouses

In Shakespeare's Twelfth Night, *Viola disguises herself as a boy called "Cesario" to serve Duke Orsino.*

Boy actors discovered that female clothes meant tight waists and stiff, uncomfortable bodices.

In this quote, Hamlet is hearing about a company of boy actors who have put the adult players out of a job. Amateur acting was part of a boy's education, and the scholars of Eton, St Paul's and Westminster were frequently invited to court to perform their plays privately for the queen. Around 1600 there developed a fashion for companies of professional child actors who performed adult plays. These companies became extremely popular, to the extent that they threatened the adult companies.

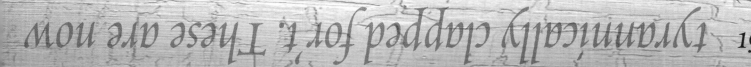

Stage, Sets and Costumes

Theatre in Shakespeare's time did not have sets or scenery. There was just an open stage, with pillars to support a platform above, called "heaven". The audience conjured up the location and the scenery in their own imagination, helped by the power of Shakespeare's descriptive language and the actors' skill. Even uneducated people were accustomed to using their imagination in this way.

> *Is it not monstrous that this player here,*
> *But in a fiction, in a dream of passion,*
> *Could force his soul so to his own conceit*
> *That from her working all his visage*
> *wann'd.*
>
> HAMLET, ACT 2, SCENE 2

but: only
conceit: thing he was imagining
visage: face
wann'd: went pale

Because there was so little scenery on stage, the actors had to hold the audience's attention by the force of their acting. Hamlet is talking here about an actor who is moved by the power of his own performance. The big open stage was bare apart from small items like chairs or tables which could be carried on. There was usually a curtain behind which characters could hide or listen unseen to other characters' conversation, when the plot demanded it.

In the floor of the stage was a trap-door, through which devils or ghosts could appear.

At the reconstructed Globe, original performances are recreated as closely as possible.

I will discharge it in either your straw-colour beard, your orange-tawny beard, your purple-in-grain beard, or your French-crown-colour beard, your perfect yellow.
A MIDSUMMER NIGHT'S DREAM, ACT 1, SCENE 2

discharge: perform
orange-tawny: tan-coloured
purple-in-grain: scarlet or crimson
French-crown: a gold coin

Costumes were very expensive. The main actors had special outfits, but the rest usually had to make do with what was in stock. Some actors wore or carried props to suggest their character — kings wore crowns, huntsmen carried bows, and so on. Characters could also be identified by the style of wig or beard they wore, which is why Bottom here is worrying about his beard.

Apart from plays like Julius Caesar, *which needed historical costume, most were probably performed in elaborate versions of Elizabethan dress.*

On Tour

The big permanent theatres only existed in London. Elsewhere in the country people still looked forward to the visits of small companies of actors who travelled around, setting up their temporary stages in inn-yards and public houses as they had for a hundred years. Touring was hard work. The actors had to carry all the costumes and props around with them on dangerous, poor-quality country roads, and lodgings were often uncomfortable.

Will you see the players well bestowed?... Let them be well used, for they are the abstract and brief chronicles of the time.

HAMLET, ACT 2, SCENE 2

bestowed: given lodgings
abstract: summary, description

The troupe of players who have arrived at court here in *Hamlet* are professionals on tour from the city. Major London companies, like Shakespeare's own, also went on tour in the summer months. Often they were forced to do this when plague broke out in London and the theatres had to close. Hamlet's visitors are lucky that he admires them and wants them taken care of, but actors weren't always welcome. Local authorities were suspicious of them because performances attracted rough company like pickpockets and other thieves.

When Shakespeare's company went on tour, they did not perform in inn-yards but in the country houses of rich families like this one.

> Here's a marvellous convenient place for our rehearsal. This green plot shall be our stage, this hawthorn-brake our tiring-house.
>
> A MIDSUMMER NIGHT'S DREAM, ACT 3, SCENE 1

brake: clump of trees
tiring-house: dressing room

The amateur players here are rehearsing outdoors, but their performance eventually takes place at court in front of the duke. Shakespeare knew all about this because his own company was often summoned to perform for Queen Elizabeth, either at court or in the houses of the various nobles she stayed with. They also played in university towns like Oxford, where *The Comedy of Errors* and *Hamlet* were performed in 1603. They were fortunate. The university authorities were choosy and some other visiting companies were paid to go away without performing!

It was a great event in a small town when a troupe of strolling players arrived to set up their stage.

Valuable costumes were always at risk on tour. Any actor tempted to wear his costume off-stage could incur a very expensive fine.

Entertainment for the Rich

Rich Elizabethans loved being entertained, but they loved taking part in events even more. Historical pageants were very popular, and also tournaments, in which knights in armour jousted on horseback. At home, theatre performances, music and dancing were favourites, along with the masque, a short, stylised verse play with dances and music, performed in costume and with elaborate scenery.

> *Come now; what masques, what dances shall we have,*
> *To wear away this long age of three hours*
> *Between our after-supper and bed-time?*
> A MIDSUMMER NIGHT'S DREAM, ACT 5, SCENE 1

Great houses provided entertainment every evening after dinner: some serious, some more light-hearted. Many households kept a permanent staff of musicians, storytellers, jugglers, acrobats and even performing animals. More serious music was provided by professionals who played the lute music of John Dowland or sang madrigals and complicated part-songs. Everyone was delighted by poetry and language. Not only was it the fashion for an aristocrat to be the patron of a struggling poet but many also wrote sonnets themselves.

Jugglers, fire-eaters and acrobats learned their trade at travelling fairs.

Between our after-supper and bed-time?

> Was ever a man had such luck? When I kissed the jack upon an up-cast, to be hit away! I had a hundred pound on't.
>
> CYMBELINE, ACT 2, SCENE 1

kissed the jack: touched the "jack" bowl
up-cast: a throw

Musicians played throughout long Elizabethan dinners, often from an upstairs gallery above the dining room.

This character in *Cymbeline* is playing bowls, a popular game for both men and women, and he's also betting on the outcome. Henry VIII and his queen, Anne Boleyn, were keen gamblers and made it fashionable. Some risked their family fortunes at card playing and dice games. The latest fashionable entertainment, the firework display, was risky in a different way. At Warwick in 1572 the impressive display set off to entertain Queen Elizabeth went badly wrong, setting fire to a house and almost killing the elderly couple inside.

The passion for playing cards and dice games attracted professional gamblers, who tricked the unwary out of their winnings.

Entertainment for the Countryfolk

Shakespeare's play *The Winter's Tale* includes a sheep-shearing festival and tells us a lot about the entertainment enjoyed by country people of his own day. While Londoners flocked to the new drama, rural districts were still enjoying old-fashioned plays from the medieval period. Their lives were largely shaped by the festivals of the church calendar and the rhythm of the seasons. Whole villages took part in the plays and entertainments that marked these events, as well as the feasting that accompanied them.

> *Methinks I play as I have seen them do*
> *In Whitsun pastorals: sure this robe of mine*
> *Does change my disposition.*
>   THE WINTER'S TALE, ACT 4, SCENE 4

disposition: character

A musician with drum and pipe features in the stained-glass window of a church.

Whitsuntide, in May, brought great festivities, including traditional plays about Robin Hood and the electing of a May Queen and King. At Christmas, bands of "mummers" went around the villages performing an old and mysterious play about St George and the dragon. Easter brought the ancient pace-egg (easter-egg) celebrations. Sheep shearing in June and the end of the autumn harvest had their own festivals of thanksgiving, with feasting and drinking.

> *O master! if you did but hear the pedlar at the door, you would never dance again after a tabor and pipe; no, the bagpipe could not move you....*
>
> THE WINTER'S TALE,
> ACT 4, SCENE 4

tabor: small drum

A day at the fair was often the only holiday working people could look forward to in their hard lives.

Poor folk loved dancing as much as the rich, but made their own music, with lively jigs and reels played on pipes and drums. The local fair, or the arrival of a travelling pedlar, brought opportunities to buy gingerbread and sweets, ribbons and trinkets. Printed texts of bawdy songs or ballads were also popular. These were a way of passing on news and were usually sensational accounts of recent murders and other gruesome events. Those who couldn't read gathered round to hear a travelling ballad singer perform them.

Pedlars travelled for miles around the countryside, carrying all their wares on their backs.

Sports and Outdoor Pursuits

Henry VIII, who excelled at everything from jousting to billiards, popularized energetic, competitive sports among the young men at court. Under Queen Elizabeth the tradition continued, with young courtiers showing off their agility and grace. They enjoyed fencing, wrestling, running races, tilting at the ring (a form of jousting), and other feats of horsemanship. Hawking and hunting, although fun, schooled men in the strategies of war. The poor also enjoyed hunting because it put extra meat on the table.

Practice in sports like fencing kept courtiers fit and trained for army service.

> *When we have matched our rackets to these balls,*
> *We will, in France, by God's grace play a set*
> *Shall strike his father's crown into the hazard.*
> HENRY V, ACT 1, SCENE 2

hazard: part of the Elizabethan tennis court where the ball is "out"

The relatively new sport of tennis was played on an indoor court on a stone floor. Henry VIII, who loved playing it, had tennis courts built in all the royal palaces, along with bowling alleys and archery butts. Ordinary people played a dangerous game of football, with a heavy leather ball and dozens of people on each team. Rich and poor alike enjoyed cruel spectacles like cockfighting, bear- and bull-baiting, violent sports which often took place right next to theatre performances.

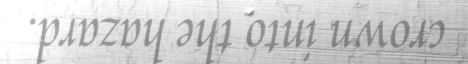
crown into the hazard.

> ... Like an arrow shot
> From a well experienc'd archer
> hits the mark
> His eye doth level at.
> PERICLES, ACT 1, SCENE 1

level: aim

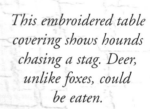

This embroidered table covering shows hounds chasing a stag. Deer, unlike foxes, could be eaten.

Some sports, like archery, skittles and billiards, could be enjoyed by both men and women. The game of darts was invented as an indoor alternative, perhaps so that archers could practise in the winter. Horse and dog racing were also popular with all classes, and provided a further opportunity for gambling. A fast horse or greyhound could make its owner rich and famous.

Tennis was a hard game because the balls, made of sheepskin stuffed with sawdust, were heavy and did not bounce well.

We will, in France, by God's

Timeline

1337-1453	The Hundred Years War, dramatized by Shakespeare in *Edward III*.
1455-1485	The Wars of the Roses, dramatized by Shakespeare in his history plays.
1533	Princess Elizabeth, daughter of King Henry VIII, is born.
1558	Elizabeth becomes queen.
1563	Plague, spreading from Europe, kills 20,000 people in London.
1564	Shakespeare is born.
1565	Tobacco is first introduced to England.
1566	London's Royal Exchange, a shopping and trading centre, is founded by Thomas Gresham.
1576	The Theatre, the first major permanent theatre, opens on the banks of the Thames, followed by the Curtain (1577), the Rose (1587), the Swan (1596), the Fortune (1599) and others.
1581	The first ballet is performed in France.
1593	Christopher Marlowe is killed in a tavern brawl.
1594	Shakespeare becomes a founder member of the Lord Chamberlain's Men.
1599	The Globe, Shakespeare's theatre, opens.
1600	The East India Company is established, opening up trade with India and the east.
1603	Death of Queen Elizabeth. On the accession of James I, Shakespeare's company is renamed the King's Men.
1613	The Globe is destroyed by fire.
1615	*The English Housewife*, cookery book and general household manual, is published.
1616	Shakespeare dies.
1618	King James' *Book of Sports* encourages the playing of various sports, to the fury of the Puritans.
1637	Ben Jonson dies.
1642	Beginning of the English Civil War closes the theatres.

Glossary

Difficult Shakespearean words appear alongside each quotation. This glossary explains words used in the main text.

apprenticed to	Assigned to study with a skilled worker in order to learn a trade.
bear- or bull-baiting	A sport in which bears or bulls were set loose to be attacked by dogs.
cockfighting	A sport in which two cockerels fought each other to the death.
cooperative	An enterprise owned jointly by all the members, who also share the profits.
fencing	The sport of fighting with swords.
gallery	A balcony with rows of seats running around the inside wall of a theatre.
hawking	Hunting with birds of prey.
Hundred Years War	A war between England and France fought between 1337 and 1453.
inn-yard	The courtyard of an inn where coaches pulled in.
jousting	Combat between two mounted knights fighting with lances.
madrigal	A song in which several people sing different parts.
morris dance	A folk dance usually danced by men wearing bells and ribbons.
mummers	Masked performers in a folk play.
pageant	An elaborate show portraying scenes from history.
patron	A sponsor or benefactor who gives financial support to artists.
pedlar	A travelling salesman.
plague	A very infectious disease.
props	Short for 'properties': the moveable items needed on stage.
prose	Ordinary language, not in rhyming lines like poetry.
Puritans	Extreme Protestants.
satirical	Ridiculing someone or something.
sonnet	A short poem of 14 lines
stock gesture	An over-used, conventional body movement.
stylized	Performed according to an established style to create a desired effect.
Wars of the Roses	The struggle for the English crown between the families of York and Lancaster (1455– 1485).

Further Information

Further Reading

The Best Loved Plays of Shakespeare by Abigail Frost and Jennifer Mulherin (Cherrytree Books, 1997)
Sightseers Shakespeare (Kingfisher Books, 2002)
Shakespeare's Storybook by Patrick Ryan (Barefoot Books, 2001)
Eyewitness: Shakespeare by Peter Chrisp (Dorling Kindersley, 2002)
Look Inside a Shakespearean Theatre by Peter Chrisp (Hodder Wayland, 2000)
The Illustrated World of the Tudors by Peter Chrisp (Hodder Wayland, 2001)
Shakespeare and the Elizabethan Age by Andrew Langley (Treasure Chest, 2000)
The Usborne World of Shakespeare by Anna Claybourne (Usborne, 2001)
What the Tudors and Stuarts Did for Us by Adam Hart-Davis (Boxtree, 2002)

Video, DVD and CD-Rom

All Shakespeare's plays are available in several versions from the Royal Shakespeare Company and can be ordered from their website (see below)
Complete Works of Shakespeare on CD-Rom (Focus Multimedia)

Websites

www.rsc.org.uk
Royal Shakespeare Company. Contains information about plays and education projects.

www.shakespeare.org.uk
Shakespeare Birthplace Trust. Contains background information on Shakespeare, his life and times.

www.shakespeares-globe.org
Shakespeare's Globe. Contains background information on Elizabethan theatre, the reconstructed building, and education projects.

Index